TRUST DEED,

FROM

ELIPHALET NOTT AND WIFE,

TO THE

TRUSTEES OF UNION COLLEGE.

To all to whom these Presents shall come:

GREETING.

ARTICLE I.

§ 1. WHEREAS under certain contracts and stipulations, made by the firm of Yates and McIntyre, with Eliphalet Nott, President of Union College, large profits accrued to the said Eliphalet Nott, in consideration of monies advanced and hazards run by him in behalf of said firm, for the purpose of protecting the interests of Union College during the drawing of certain Lotteries which belonged to said firm, in some of which Lotteries Union College was interested; a portion of which profits has been expended in the enlargement and improvement of the College site, or the buildings thereon erected, or in the furtherance of those arts and sciences which it is the object of the said institution to promote, and a portion of which profits, as well as certain amounts from other private sources, have from time to time been deposited by the said Eliphalet Nott with the Treasurer of Union College, under and in pursuance of certain resolutions of the Trustees of said College; and other portions of which profits, as well as certain amounts from other private sources, have been expended in the purchase of certain real estate in the City of New-York and on Long Island, which said deposits and real estate, after providing for expenses, liabilities and losses incurred in the transaction of the business, being intended by the said Eliphalet Nott, as repeatedly declared by him in official reports to the said Trustees, to be bestowed on Union College, or some

Contracts of Yates & McIntyre with E. Nott.

Portion of profits expended on College building and site.

Other portions deposited with Treasurer.

Other portions invested in real estate to be bestowed on Union College.

kindred institution connected therewith, at such times, in such manner, and for such purposes as the said Eliphalet Nott should direct.

Trustees convey Stuyvesant Cove and Hunter Farm to E. Nott.

§ 2. And the said deposits having increased to a large amount, and the said Trustees having become the owners of the Stuyvesant Cove property, and of one-half of the Hunter Farm, directed the conveyance of the same to the said Eliphalet Nott, and paid him the sum of $46,649.85, including interest, in part satisfaction of the said deposits, still leaving a balance of the said deposits in favor of the said Eliphalet Nott.

Exchanges of property.

§ 3. And whereas there have also been divers pecuniary transactions and exchanges of securities with Union College, by the said Eliphalet Nott, relating chiefly and almost entirely to the monies so deposited by him, which sums of money so received by the said Eliphalet Nott were chiefly if not wholly employed in meeting the liabilities incurred in the purchase of the Stuyvesant Cove property, and Hunter Farm, or other properties intended for the ultimate benefit of Union College, or some kindred institution connected therewith, or in removing incumbrances thereon, or in the improvement and enhancement of the value of the same, or in meeting the losses connected with and springing out of the management thereof.

Deed of Trust heretofore executed.

§ 4. And whereas the said Eliphalet Nott in execution of his said original design, has heretofore executed a deed of trust to Union College and for its benefit, of his remaining interest in the Stuyvesant Cove property, after providing for the incumbrances thereon and the liabilities of Hezekiah Bradford, subject to which the said Eliphalet Nott received the title thereto from Diodate Brainerd, and also his remaining interest in the entire Hunter Farm, the Griffin Farm, the undivided half of the Provost Farm, the Devoe Meadow and the Van Alst Farm, as set forth in an agreement made on the 28th day of December, 1852, between Jonathan Crane and Charles Ely, of the first part, and the said Eliphalet Nott, of the second part, and deposited the same with the Treasurer of Union College to be delivered at the death of the said Eliphalet Nott, and has also by his last will and testament confirmed the said conveyance.

§ 5. And whereas the Treasurer of Union College by and with the consent and approbation of the Finance Committee, or Eliphalet Nott, the chairman thereof, did at various times make loans and investments of its funds, some of which are supposed to be of little value, but which were made in good faith.

Profits on lands in Schenectady.

§ 6. And whereas large gains and profits have accrued to the said College from the purchase of lands in and about Schenectady, by the private means of the said Eliphalet Nott, and the sale of said lands at advanced prices, in which gains the said Eliphalet Nott has in no instance consented to share, and the whole of which has therefore enured to the benefit of Union College.

Final settlement.

§ 7. And whereas the said Eliphalet Nott has supposed that his repeated declarations, and his official reports to the Trustees of Union College in relation to the ultimate disposition of the said deposit fund, operated effectually to divest him of all claim thereto, when a full settlement of his accounts with Union College should be had according to the terms of the resolutions of the Trustees; and such being now made and consummated as hereinafter stated.

Considerations.

§ 8. Therefore, in consideration of the premises, and of a full, entire and final settlement of all accounts, claims and demands at law or in equity, between the said College and the said Eliphalet Nott, as evidenced by this instrument, and a certain other instrument, on the part of the said College to the said Eliphalet Nott, executed and delivered cotemporaneously with this instrument, and both instruments forming parts of the same transaction.

Grant of balance due E. Nott on account of deposit fund.

§ 9. I, the said Eliphalet Nott, in further execution of the said original design, and to attain immediately the objects and purposes of the said deed of trust, do hereby give, grant, transfer and assign to the corporation known as the Trustees of Union College, in the town of Schenectady, in the State of New-York, the balance now due or appearing to be due on the books of the said College or otherwise, whatever it may be, of the deposits so made by me as aforesaid, with the Treasurer of Union College, or received by him for my benefit, in part or in whole; and I do hereby release and forever discharge the said Trustees of Union College from all claims, demands, actions and causes of action, for or on account of the said deposits, or the interest thereon; or for or on account of any gifts or donations to the said College; and from all claims of any monies paid to or received by the said College, growing or arising from or on account of certain stipulations of the firm of Yates and McIntyre, of January 4th and January 24th, 1826.

II.

ARTICLE II.

§ 10. And in further execution of his said original design, and for the purpose of confirming the objects of the said deed of trust hereinbefore mentioned, and of giving immediate effect to the said original design, so as to obviate all doubts that may arise thereon, and in consideration of the premises and matters hereinbefore stated, I, the said Eliphalet Nott, do hereby assign, give, transfer, sell and convey to the said Trustees of Union College, in the town (now city) of Schenectady, in trust, and for the uses and purposes hereinafter declared, the Bonds, Mortgages and Securities specified and enumerated in a Schedule hereto annexed, marked A, signed by me, and constituting a part of this instrument: which Bonds, Mortgages and Securities have also been separately assigned to the said College, by proper assignments endorsed on them respectively, or attached to them; and also all the right, title, and interest of the said Eliphalet Nott in an agreement made the 28th day in December, 1852, between Jonathan Crane and Charles Ely, of the first part, and the said Eliphalet Nott, of the second part, and in the premises, property, rights and interests therein mentioned or described, a copy of which agreement is contained in a Schedule also hereunto annexed, marked B, and signed by me, and which has also been separately assigned by me to the said College, subject to all the stipulations therein contained, which assignments, transfers, sales and conveyance are made IN TRUST for the uses and purposes hereinafter particularly specified, and subject to the powers in trust hereinafter reserved to the said Eliphalet Nott and declared by him, and which are recognised, declared and confirmed in the said instrument executed by the Trustees of Union College, and delivered cotemporaneously with this instrument.

Grant of securities in schedule A.

Securities separately assigned.

Grant of agreement with Crane & Ely.

III.

ARTICLE III.

§ 11. The following are the powers in trust which the said Eliphalet Nott reserves to himself, to be executed by him in relation to the property, rights and interests described in the aforesaid agreement between him and Jonathan Crane and Charles Ely, contained in Sche-

Powers in trust reserved by grantor.

dule B, hereto annexed and by this instrument conveyed to Union College, so long as in his judgment the exercise of the said powers shall be necessary to fulfill the covenants and stipulations on his part contained in said agreement, and to place the real property described in the said agreement in the most advantageous condition for sale or lease. The said powers in trust so reserved hereby, are the following:

§ 12. *First.* To superintend, control and direct the management and care of the real estate described in the said agreement, and the preparing the same for use, and in vending and disposing thereof for the common benefit of the said Crane and Ely, and Union College, so far as the said agreement authorises such superintendence, management and control by the said Eliphalet Nott and his assigns. Right of superintending.

§ 13. *Second.* To examine and settle the accounts for expenditures and outlays made by the said Crane and Ely, upon or by reason of the property aforesaid; and also of the monies received by them therefrom, or from any sales, lease, or mortgage, or other disposition of the same. Of examining and settling accounts.

§ 14. *Third.* To receive from the said Crane and Ely the one-third part of all monies collected and received by them, or which ought to be collected by them, as aforesaid, after the directions specified in the said agreement; and to receive from the said Crane and Ely, assignments and transfers of the one-third of all bonds, mortgages, securities, engagements and property of whatever kind and nature, received and acquired by the said Crane and Ely, or either of them, out of or by reason of the premises mentioned in the said agreement, or of the sales, leasing, mortgage or other disposition of the said property, rights and interests, or any part thereof; which assignments and transfers are to be made to the said Union College, subject to the trusts herein declared, and which monies when not retained and applied to the purpose in the fifth subdivision of the said agreement mentioned, are to be paid over to the Treasurer of Union College to be invested in the manner and for the uses and purposes hereinafter declared. To receive and pay Treasurer monies and securities.

§ 15. *Fourth.* To receive one-third of all net profits of any and of all contracts made by the said Crane and Ely, or either of them for their services, or for those of any machine they may have, own or control in any dredging, grading, docking, filling, regulating, or otherwise To receive one-third of profits accruing from all contracts of Crane & Ely, and pay same to Treasurer.

preparing for use or sale, any of the lands mentioned in the said agreement, or any other adjoining or neighboring thereto; which monies are to be paid over to the Treasurer of Union College, to be invested in the manner and for the uses and purposes hereinafter declared.

To receive conveyances.

§ 16. *Fifth.* To demand and to receive of the said Crane and Ely, whenever, and as often he shall deem it expedient, conveyances of one-third part of so much of the premises mentioned in the said agreement as may not have been sold, and to comply with the terms specified in the Seventh article of the said agreement. And in order to fulfill such terms, when the payment of any money is necessary, in order to be entitled to any conveyance, to retain out of any monies received by him from the said Crane and Ely sufficient for that purpose and apply the same in making such payment; which conveyances are to be taken in the name and for the benefit of the Trustees of Union College, subject to the trusts, and for the uses and purposes hereinafter declared.

IV. TRUSTS.

ARTICLE IV.

Trusts on which property conveyed.

§ 17. The trusts for and upon which the aforesaid property, rights and interests are conveyed to the said Trustees, and the uses and purposes to which the same shall be devoted, and to which the income thereof shall be applied, are the following:

§ 18. Of the said property, rights and interests so conveyed, the bonds, mortgages and securities hereby assigned, and those that may be received by the Treasurer of Union College, by virtue of the aforesaid agreement with Messrs. Crane and Ely, and those that may be taken on the investment of any money that may be received under the said agreement, or on the investment of the proceeds of the sale of any land conveyed to Union College under the said agreement, and those that may be taken or received on the renewal of or change in the said investments and securities, or on the investment of any money collected or received on the said securities, are to be appropriated to the following thirteen first enumerated trusts, and the net income thereof, after paying the charges hereinafter specified, is to be applied as directed in the following specification of the said trusts, with a discretion to be exercised by the said Trustees and the Visitors hereinafter mentioned in relation to the order or priority of the application of the said income, or of any part or portion thereof, to the said particular trusts, and to the order

How monies to be appropriated

Application of income.

or priority of the appropriations of the capital of the said property, rights and interests or of any part thereof, to the foundations of the said particular trusts, or to any part of such respective foundations; and also to the application of the surplus income of any particular trust fund not required for the purposes of such fund to the specific objects of any one or more of the other of said particular trusts.

Nine professorships.

§ 19. *First.* A principal sum of the said bonds, mortgages and securities, amounting to Two Hundred and Twenty-Five Thousand Dollars, shall always be devoted to the establishment and maintenance of Nine Professorships in the said College, to each of which shall be assigned a salary of Fifteen Hundred Dollars annually; and the net income of the said principal sum only shall be applied to the payment of the said salaries in quarter yearly installments.

Six assistant professorships.

§ 20. *Second.* A principal sum of the said bonds, mortgages and securities, amounting to Sixty Thousand Dollars, shall always be devoted to the establishment and maintenance of Six Assistant Professorships in the said College, to each of which shall be assigned a salary of Six Hundred Dollars annually; and the net income of the said principal sum only shall always be applied to the payment of the said salaries in quarter yearly installments.

Astronomical observatory.

§ 21. *Third.* A principal sum of the said bonds, mortgages and securities, amounting to Sixty Thousand Dollars, shall always be devoted to establish and maintain an Astronomical Observatory for the use of the said College; and the net income of the said principal sum only shall always be used and applied in the erection or preparation of a suitable building or place for an Astronomical Observatory, or other buildings connected therewith, on ground to be conveyed by the said Eliphalet Nott to the said College for that purpose, or elsewhere; in the purchase of the necessary apparatus for the same, in the preservation and repair of said buildings and apparatus, and in the compensation of the necessary observers, assistants, laborers, and other necessary persons employed in the said Observatory.

Sixty auxiliary scholarships in two classes.

§ 22. *Fourth.* A principal sum of the said bonds, mortgages and securities, amounting to Twenty Thousand Dollars, shall always be devoted to the establishment and maintenance of Sixty Auxiliary Scholarships in said College, to be divided into two classes, of Thirty Scholarships each, to be denominated respectively the First and Second Class of Auxiliary Scholarships. To the incumbents of the first class shall be paid a stipend of Ten Dollars for each college term; and to the incumbent of the Second Class shall be paid a stipend of Twelve Dollars for each college term; and the net income of said principal sum only shall always be applied to the payment of said stipends to the incumbents of said Scholarships. These Scholarships are to be awarded to the most deserving among those receiving or requiring material aid in the prosecution of their studies, of which satisfactory evidence must be furnished to the President.

First class stipeud $10.

Second class stipend $12.

Sixty prize scholarships in two classes.

§ 23. *Fifth.* A principal sum of the said bonds, mortgages and securities, amounting to Sixty Thousand Dollars, shall always be devoted to the establishment and maintenance of Sixty Prize Scholarships for undergraduates in said College, to be divided into two classes of Thirty Scholarships each, to be denominated respectively the third and fourth class of Prize Scholarships. To the incumbents of the third class shall be paid a stipend of Fifteen Dollars for each college term; and to the incumbents of the fourth class shall be paid a stipend of Eighteen Dollars for each college term; and the net income of said principal sum only shall always be applied to the payment of said stipends to the incumbents of said Scholarships. The stipends paid to twelve of the incumbents of said Prize Scholarships for undergruduates (to be selected by the President), may be increased to Twenty-Four Dollars per term, and paid them for three years after they shall have graduated; provided they shall continue during that time to prosecute at Union College the prescribed course of higher studies, (should such course be prescribed, which the wants of the country seem to require), and to perform such monitorial or other duties, as shall be required by the President; or that number of prime scholars who have already graduated may be selected by the President to fill that number of said selected Prize Scholarships, the incumbents of which in either event shall be entitled to attend lectures and recitations, and to receive books from the libraries of the College free of expense, and they may be continued on said foundation for a longer time than three years, and receive an additional compensation, if the President of College shall so recommend.

Third class $15.

Fourth class $18.

May be increased to $24.

§ 24. *Sixth.* A principal sum of the said bonds, mortgages and securities, amounting to Forty-Five Thousand Dollars, shall always be devoted to the establishment and maintenance of Nine Prize Scholarships for Graduates or Fellows in said College, to each of which there shall be assigned an annual stipend of Three Hundred Dollars; and the net income of said principal sum only shall always be applied to the payment of said stipends in quarter yearly payments.

Nine prize scholarships for graduates.

Stipend $300.

§ 25. *Seventh.* A principal sum of the said bonds, mortgages and securities, amounting to Twenty Thousand Dollars, shall always be devoted to the preparation and maintenance of ground to be conveyed to the said Trustees by the said E. Nott, for a Cemetery, for the use of the said College, and for the burial therein of such persons and on such terms as the said Trustees and Visitors shall allow; and the net income of the said principal sum only shall always be applied for the purposes herein indicated, and for the improvement of the grounds connected with such Cemetery.

Cemetery.

§ 26. *Eighth.* A principal sum of the said bonds, mortgages and securities, amounting to Ten Thousand Dollars, shall always be devoted to the purchase and preservation of Philosophical, Mathematical, and Chemical Apparatus for the use of said College, and the Professors, Pupils and Teachers thereof; and the net income of said principal sum only shall always be applied to the purchase, preservation and repair of such Philosophical, Mathematical and Chemical Apparatus, or of Apparatus required in the Engineering Department.

Purchase of apparatus.

§ 27. *Ninth.* A principal sum of the said bonds, mortgages and securities, amounting to Five Thousand Dollars, shall always be devoted to the procuring of Text Books for the use of the Students in said College, on such terms, (except as herein otherwise directed,) as the Trustees and Visitors hereinafter named shall prescribe; and the net income of the said principal sum only shall always be applied to the procuring and furnishing such Text Books.

Purchase of text books.

§ 28. *Tenth.* A principal sum of the said bonds, mortgages and securities, amounting to Thirty Thousand Dollars, shall always be devoted to the purchase of Scientific, Classical, Philosophical, Theological, Medical and Law Books, for the establishment of an Eclectic Library in the said College, for the use of the Officers, Teachers and

Eclectic library.

Pupils therein: and the net income of the said principal sum only shall always be applied to the purchase of Books for the said Library, and to the preservation and maintenance of the same.

Geological and mineral cabinet.

§ 29. *Eleventh.* A principal sum of the said bonds, mortgages and securities, amounting to Five Thousand Dollars, shall always be devoted to the establishment and maintenance of a Cabinet of Geological Specimens, especially Fossil and Mineral Specimens of the United States and State of New-York, for the use of Union College; and the net income of said principal sum only shall always be applied to that object.

Historical cabinet.

§ 30. *Twelfth.* A principal sum of the said bonds, mortgages and securities, amounting to Five Thousand Dollars, shall always be devoted to the establishment and maintenance of a Cabinet of Historical Medals, Coins, Maps, Paintings and other Historical Memorials for the use of Union College; and the net income of said principal sum only shall always be applied to the purchase and keeping of such articles.

Lecture fund.

§ 31. *Thirteenth.* A principal sum of the said bonds, mortgages and securities, amounting to Ten Thousand Dollars, shall always be devoted to the procurement of occasional Lectures for the Students of Union College, particularly on the dangers and duties of youth, especially of Students; the development and preservation of the physical, intellectual and moral constitution of man, the preservation of health, and on the laws of life; and the net income of the said principal sum only shall always be applied to that object.

Miscellaneous fund.

§ 32. *Fourteenth.* The principal sum of the residue of the said bonds, mortgages and securities not devoted to any of the preceding objects and purposes, and of the property, rights and interests under the aforesaid agreement with Messrs. Crane and Ely, hereby conveyed to the said Trustees, which shall be at any time undisposed of, shall be designated the Miscellaneous Fund, and shall be always devoted to the following purposes; and the income, rents and profits thereof only shall be applied to the same purposes, namely:

Expenses to be paid.

1. To pay the expenses of executing any of the foregoing trusts, and the taxes, liens, assessments and incumbrances on any of the property hereby conveyed, the insurance on any buildings erected on the real property acquired under the said agreements, and to pay the compensation of the Visitors for their services hereinafter directed.

2. To make up and supply any deficiencies that may exist in the income of any of the said principal sums hereinbefore devoted to specific purposes, so as to secure the attainment of the said objects and purposes. Deficiencies to be made up.

3. The residue of the said income shall be applied in the discretion of the Trustees of the said College and the Visitors hereinafter mentioned, to any or either of the aforesaid specified objects and purposes, and to no other use or purpose ; but in such application preference may be given to the increase of the number of Professorships, Assistant Professorships or Scholarships; and also to the increase of the respective salaries and stipends of the Professorships, Assistant Professorships, or Scholarships, directed to be established by this deed of trust, or the salary or stipend of any one of them, should this in the judgment of the Trustees and Visitors be deemed expedient. Application of residue.

§ 33. If at any time the principal of the aforesaid trust estate shall from any cause be diminished, then that diminution shall be made up by the accumulation of the income of all the aforesaid specific appropriations, except that the income appropriated to the support of Professorships, Assistant Professorships and Scholarships, shall be accumulated only while they are vacant; and by adding the amount thus accumulated to the remaining capital till the same, with such addition, shall be equal to the capital as it originally existed ; but this direction is not to take effect until an act of the Legislature can be obtained for that purpose. Diminution in principal, how to be made up.

ARTICLE V.

V. ACCOUNTS.

§ 34. The following conditions are to be observed in relation to the investments, management and accounts of the funds hereby instituted : Conditions.

§ 35. All monies received as principal from any of the property, rights and interests hereby conveyed, or from the avails thereof, are to be invested as speedily as may be consistent with their safety, in permanent securities; and until such investments be made, such monies may be deposited with some savings or other bank in good credit, upon the best rates of interest that can be obtained. The interest thus received on deposits previous to permanent investment, shall be deemed and considered a part of the income or revenue of the Miscellaneous Monies to be invested as fast as received.

Fund hereinbefore mentioned and enumerated as the Fourteenth Trust, and shall be applied to the objects and in the manner directed in respect to the income of that fund.

Manner of investment.

§ 36. The principal sums of the property, rights and interests hereby conveyed, when not already invested, shall be invested in bonds and mortgages on unincumbered real estate in agricultural districts, worth at least one-third more than the amount exclusive of buildings; or on unincumbered real estate in any city, worth, with the insurance of the buildings thereon, at least one-third more than the amount invested; or in the public stocks of the United States, or of the State of New-York, or of Massachusetts, Connecticut, Ohio, or Pennsylvania; or in the bonds or stocks of the City of New-York, or of the City of Albany, or Troy, the bonds of the New-York Central railroad company, by the Treasurer of Union College, under the direction of the Trustees and Visitors hereinafter appointed, or of such committee, or of at least two members thereof, as such Trustees and Visitors shall appoint for this purpose. And such investments may also be made by the said Treasurer, under such direction, in such other securities as shall be authorized by the highest court having original jurisdiction in the district in which the city of Schenectady is situated.

Accounts to be kept distinct.

§ 37. The securities hereby conveyed, and those that may be received or taken by the Treasurer or Trustees of said College, shall be entered in a book or books, in which shall also be entered a statement of all other property received or acquired by virtue of this conveyance, which books shall be entirely distinct from the books of account of the other property and funds of Union College; and every such book shall contain a printed copy of this deed bound in the same. The payments of principal and interest on any security, shall be entered in the said books, and the reinvestment of any principal sums received on any security, shall be so entered as to refer to the security on which it was paid, as far as practicable, to the end that every security may be traced on the said accounts, whatever form of investment it may assume. There shall also be entered in said books, all the reports of the Treasurer of Union College to the Trustees, and the reports of Finance and Examining Committees, and the proceedings of the Trustees and Visitors in relation to the funds and property hereby conveyed, and the condition and application thereof, to which Books the Visitors shall at all times have free access.

§ 38. If the income or revenue of the Miscellaneous Fund hereinbefore instituted and enumerated as the Fourteenth, shall at any time be insufficient to pay any taxes or assessments legally charged upon any property hereby conveyed, then the same shall be paid out of the income of the fund to which the property, liable to such taxes or assessments may belong, and the same shall be charged upon the said income. Taxes, &c. how to be paid.

§ 39. If at any time the revenue of the said Miscellaneous Fund, enumerated as the Fourteenth, shall be insufficient to pay the compensation hereinafter provided for the Visitors hereinafter appointed, or to defray the expenses of executing the trusts hereby created, then the amount of such deficiency shall be paid out of the income of all the funds hereby instituted, which shall at the time be yielding income. Provision for payment of visitors.

ARTICLE VI.

VI.

§ 40. The property, rights and interests, hereby granted and conveyed, are to be subject to visitation according to the following provisions: Subject to visitation.

§ 41. There shall be at first six Visitors. The said Eliphalet Nott, Urania E. Nott, Bishop Alonzo Potter, the Rev. John Nott, Judge William W. Campbell, and Richard M. Blatchford, Esq., shall be Visitors during their natural lives; and the number of their successors in office, and the filling of vacancies as they occur, shall be provided for in perpetuity in such manner as the said Eliphalet Nott shall prescribe in an instrument signed and acknowledged by him, and filed with the Treasurer of the Trustees of Union College, who shall cause the same to be printed and attached to and preserved with the printed copies of this trust deed, in the several books in which the same is bound. But in case such provision shall not be made by the said Eliphalet Nott, then the persons respectively who shall at the time be installed Ministers of the First Presbyterian Church in the city of Schenectady, of the First Reformed Dutch Church in the city of Schenectady, of the First Protestant Episcopal Church in the city of Schenectady, of the First Congregational Church in the city of Albany, and of the First Presbyterian Church in the

Number of visitors.

Appointment of successors to be provided for.

If not provided for, visitors to be ex-officio.

city of Troy, shall be Visitors during their continuance as such ministers, to be succeeded as Visitors in perpetuity by their respective successors as ministers in the said churches. As vacancies occur in the Board of Visitors composed of the persons hereinbefore specially named, the first five of the said vacancies are to be supplied by the said ministers, in the order in which they are herein enumerated; and the presiding Justice of the Supreme Court in the Judicial District in which the city of Schenectady is situated, when a sixth vacancy shall occur in the Board of Visitors composed of the persons herein first named, shall become an ex-officio Visitor during his term of office, to be succeeded in perpetuity by his successors during their respective terms of office. And in case of the abolition of the office, or a change in the organization of the Judiciary, by which there shall be no presiding Justice, then the senior Judge of the highest Court of Law and Equity having original jurisdiction in the District in which the city of Schenectady shall be situated, shall become an ex-officio Visitor during his term of office, to be succeeded in perpetuity by his successors during their respective terms of office. And in case of the refusal of any of the persons herein designated as Visitors to act, or in case of there being no such persons to act, then the Governor of the State may appoint proper persons to fill such vacancies.

Vacancies, order in which to be filled.

Governor may appoint in certain cases.

§ 42. To each of the first six Visitors above named, shall be paid in quarterly payments by the Treasurer of Union College, out of the income hereinbefore provided for that purpose, as follows, to wit: to Urania E. Nott, Bishop Alonzo Potter and the Rev. John Nott, Two hundred dollars severally for each year's service; to E. Nott, nothing; to Judge William W. Campbell and Richard M. Blatchford, Esq., as well as to each and all of the ex-officio successors of the six first named Visitors forever, in addition to their necessary travelling expenses, the sum of Three Dollars per day for each day they shall be employed in attending the meeting of the Board of Trustees or Visitors, or in attending the public examinations in Union College, or any other prescribed duty. As evidence of the amount of the expense so incurred, and of the number of days so employed, they shall severally present to the Treasurer from time to time a bill thereof audited by the President of the college, or some member of the Finance

Compensation of visitors.

Evidence on which payment to be made.

or other auditing committee appointed for that purpose; but to no Visitor shall the Treasurer pay more than Two Hundred Dollars for one year's service.

§ 43. And should the said Urania E. Nott survive the said Eliphalet Nott, she shall, in addition to her compensation as Visitor aforesaid, be provided with a suitable residence on the college premises, or elsewhere should she desire it, the expense of which to be defrayed out of the said Miscellaneous Fund. U. E. Nott to be provided with residence.

§ 44. The Visitors hereinbefore named, as well as those becoming Visitors ex-officio, shall be considered by the said Trustees as Visitors of Union College in respect to the trust funds hereby created, with power to discharge all the duties herein directed. Visitors to be recognized by trustees.

§ 45. Every Visitor, except the said E. Nott and the said Urania E. Nott, shall before entering upon the duties of his office, take and subscriber an affirmation (the same being previously recorded in one of the Books of Record to be provided and kept by the said Trustees for the insertion therein of all their transactions in relation to said trust funds, and the several foundations instituted thereby) in the words following, to wit: Visitors to make affirmation.

§ 46. I solemnly affirm that I will read over at intervals, and at least once a year, so much of this deed as is requisite to the full understanding of the duties of Visitors as set forth therein; and that I will well and truly execute those duties, and see as far as in me lies, that said trust is duly executed on the part of the Trustees of Union College. And in case the said Trustees shall at any time neglect to execute said trust in good faith, and according to the true intent of the said Eliphalet Nott as declared in this deed, that I will then and in that case, forthwith take such legal or other steps as may be necessary to compel on the part of the said Trustees an execution of said trust, and the necessary expenses so incurred shall be paid out of the income of the Miscellaneous Fund. Form of affirmation.

§ 47. It shall be the duty of the said Visitors, with the exception of the said Urania E. Nott, to attend the annual meeting of the Board of Trustees, when a report of the Treasurer in relation to the state of such trust fund shall be exhibited to said Visitors for their examination; and it shall also be the duty of such Visitors from time to Visitors to attend meetings of trustees.

To examine into state of funds.

time to examine into the state of said trust fund, and the several foundations arising therefrom, and to see that the same is properly invested, and the income thereof applied as hereinbefore directed. It shall also be their duty to see that a correct and detailed report of the condition of the principal of the said trust funds is made annually to the Regents of the University, together with a statement of the application of the income for the preceding year; and in case the Board of Regents shall be dissolved, to see that such report be made annually to the Legislature.

To see that annual reports are made.

To attend examinations.

§ 48. It shall also be their duty, especially after the death of the said E. Nott, to attend the several examinations of the classes in said College, and to see that no immoral, incompetent or negligent incumbent of any Scholarship is permitted to continue to receive the stipend attached to the same; and to enable Visitors understandingly to discharge this duty, they must be furnished by the Register or other proper officer, at the close of each term, with a statement of the attainments and attendance of each incumbent of the Auxiliary or Prize Scholarships for undergraduates during the preceding term. Or, if preferred, said Visitors, or a committee thereof, may, for said purpose, meet the incumbents of the Auxiliary Scholarships and of the Prize Scholarships during the term, and in view of their attendance, application and progress, address to them such words of counsel, rebuke or encouragement, as their several cases may require. And such visitation of said Scholarships during term time, should in any event occasionally be had by said Visitors or some member or committee appointed for that purpose.

Visitors to constitute separate board.

§ 49. So long as the said E. Nott shall continue to act as Visitor, the said Visitors shall in all cases constitute a separate Board, and the acts of a majority shall be deemed the acts of the Board; and thereafter the Trustees and Visitors shall meet and act together as one Board in those cases in which their joint action is required by this instrument, and the majority of the joint votes of said Board, provided two Visitors are present, shall be final.

Trustees and visitors to act together.

Visitors to meet separately once a year.

§ 50. The Visitors are required to meet as a separate Board at least once a year, at the College in Schenectady, when in addition to the appointments of the requisite committees and the transaction of other business,the following questions shall be put, and a vote taken on each; and the names of the persons voting shall be entered:

1. Are the funds which we as Visitors are to supervise safely and well invested?

2. Are the Trustees of Union College executing in good faith the trusts committed to them by the trust deed of E. Nott and U. E. Nott?

3. Are the Professors and Assistant Professors or Tutors, who derive any benefit from the said deed, keeping their pledges, discharging their respective duties with fidelity, and sustaining a good moral character?

4. Are the Prize Students keeping their pledges, studying diligently, attending the College exercises with punctuality, and sustaining a good moral character?

§ 51. The action had each year on these several questions, as well as all other acts of the Visitors, shall be recorded and preserved in a book of minutes provided for that purpose, and attested by the Chairman or Secretary of the Board. Records to be kept.

ARTICLE VII.

VII.

§ 52. The following conditions and regulations respecting the Professorships and Assistant Professorships, the appointment of incumbents, the designation of their duties, and their removal, are to be observed: Appointment, &c. of professors.

§ 53. When the income herein provided for Professors and Assistant Professors shall be adequate, they shall be appointed by the concurrent act of the Board of Trustees of Union College and of the Visitors, while the said Eliphalet Nott acts as a Visitor; either of which Boards may nominate to the other; and when he ceases to act as Visitor, then the said appointments shall be made by the said Trustees and the Visitors, in joint meeting, or by a majority of them; and when any vacancy occurs in any Professorship or Assistant Professorship, said vacancy shall be filled in the manner above prescribed for the appointment of Professors and Assistant Professors. How to be made.

§ 54. In order to distinguish the Professorships and Assistant Professorships founded by this instrument, they shall severally be numbered, and each shall be distinguished by its appropriate number in Professorships how distinguished.

connection with such additional terms of designation as may be directed by the Trustees of Union College and the Visitors.

Duties to be prescribed by trustees and visitors.

§ 55. The duties appertaining to the Professorships and Assistant Professorships founded by this instrument, shall be prescribed by the Trustees of Union College and the Visitors, and the same may be varied and modified in their discretion; and they may be employed not only as teachers in the College, or in preparatory schools, but also as Librarians, Registers, Treasurers, and Keepers of Reading, Geological and other public rooms; and more than one Professorship or Assistant Professorship, may be temporarily assigned to the same person, or an additional compensation may be annexed to the same Professorship or Assistant Professorship, whenever, from the desire of securing the services of some distinguished man, or on account of the nature of the service to be performed, or for any other reason, the Trustees and Visitors shall so determine; or the compensation of any Professor, Assistant Professor, or Fellow, may be diminished on account of absences, infirmity, the less onerous nature or the shorter term of service annually required to be performed, or for any other reason, if the Trustees and Visitors shall so determine.

Additional compensation.

Compensation may be diminished.

Assistant professors to be unmarried men, except, &c.

§ 56. The incumbents of the Assistant Professorships are always to be unmarried men, and to reside in the College, unless for special and urgent reasons the Trustees and Visitors shall otherwise determine, or unless employed as teachers in preparatory schools, established in the city of Schenectady or elsewhere, should it be deemed for the interest of the College to establish such schools, in conformity to the law authorizing the same. And it shall be the duty of the said Trustees and Visitors to contribute to the establishment and permanent maintenance of at least two such schools by assigning to each a Professor or Assistant Professor of Union College, to act as principal thereof, provided the said E. Nott shall so direct, and file such direction with the Secretary of the Board of Trustees, fixing the time when, and designating the place where, such schools shall be established; and the conditions on which the pupils taught in such schools shall be admitted to the respective classes in Union College for which they are prepared.

Preparatory schools to be established, when.

President to recommend payment of extra compensation.

§ 57. It shall be the duty of the President of Union College to recommend to the Trustees and Visitors to pay to any Professor, Assistant Professor, or incumbent of any Prize Scholarship for graduates, such reasonable extra compensation as he shall approve, for any extra service which they may be respectively required to perform, which may be paid in the discretion of the Trustees and Visitors out of the income of the Miscellaneous Fund.

Disuse of tobacco recommended.

§ 58. It is earnestly recommended to and expected of every Professor, to avoid the use of tobacco in any of its forms; and each Professor before entering on the duties of his office, shall subscribe the following declaration in the book to be provided as aforesaid, to wit:

Pledge of professors.

§ 59. I solemnly promise that I will not use spirituous liquors of any kind as a beverage, so long as I shall continue to receive the avails of a Professorship founded by the deed of trust executed by Eliphalet Nott and Urania E. Nott to the Trustees of Union College, bearing date the 28th day of December, 1853, and that I will discourage the use of such liquors by others.

Assistant professors.

§ 60. And each Assistant Professor, before entering on the duties of his office, shall subscribe in the book to be provided therefore, a declaration in the words following, to wit:

Pledge.

§ 61. I solemnly promise that I will neither use tobacco in any of its forms, nor spirituous liquors of any kind as a beverage, so long as I shall continue to receive the avails of an Assistant Professorship founded by the deed of trust executed by Eliphalet Nott and Urania E. Nott to the Trustees of Union College, bearing date the 28th day of December, 1853, and that I will discourage the use of such articles by others.

Removal of professors, &c.

§ 62. Professors and Assistant Professors appointed as aforesaid, may be removed at any time by the concurrent act of the Board of Trustees of Union College and of the Visitors, while the said Eliphalet Nott contiuues to act as Visitor, either of which Boards may originate a proposition to that effect to the other Board; and when the said E. Nott shall cease to act as Visitor, then such removal may be made by the vote of a majority of said Trustees and Visitors in joint meeting.

ARTICLE VIII.

VIII. Scholarships.

§ 63. The following regulations and conditions are to be observed in relation to Auxiliary Scholarships, Prize Scholarships for undergraduates, and Prize Scholarships for graduates.

Duty of visitors to appoint examinations of candidates.

§ 64. It shall be the duty of the Visitors at their annual meeting, in each year, to designate at least one examiner from their own number, or from the Faculty, whose duty it shall be in connection with such members of the Faculty, or other persons, as the President shall designate, to examine and certify to the qualifications of candidates for the Auxiliary and Prize Scholarships as herein provided for. And they may also appoint examiners not connected with the College to attend the examinations had at the close of the several Terms, who may be paid the same per diem compensation for their attendance directed to be paid the Visitors and upon the same evidence and from the income of the same fund.

Qualifications for first stipend.

§ 65. To be entitled to the FIRST stipend, (being a stipend of the AUXILIARY SCHOLARSHIPS), the candidate must not only require material aid, but must also be *well* prepared for the class he proposes to enter; to be entitled to the SECOND stipend the candidate must not only require material aid, but must also be more than ordinarily well prepared for the class he proposes to enter, and possess talents that give promise of more than ordinary usefulness.

Second stipend.

Third stipend.

§ 66. To be entitled to the THIRD stipend, (being a stipend of the Prize Scholarships for undergraduates), the candidate must be a prime scholar and possess superior talents; and to be entitled to the FOURTH stipend, the candidate must be pre-eminent in both scholarship and talents.

Fourth stipend.

Certificate to be given.

§ 67. To which stipend the candidates examined are severally entitled, must be indicated to the President, by the examining committee, in the certificate given to them severally.

Tuition and use of text books free.

§ 68. Incumbents of whatever foundation, if in need of material aid, will, on furnishing evidence thereof to the President, be entitled, in addition to their respective stipends, to receive their Tuition and the use of their Text Books, (with the exception of Lexicons and Dictionaries which they are supposed to possess,) from the Library free of charge, unless for damage done said books while in their possession.

Incumbents may be transferred.

§ 69. The incumbents of all the several foundations may be transferred from one foundation to another, either ascending or descending, during their College course, according as they are progressive, stationary or retrograde, if the Visitors shall, by their own act, or by a committee, so determine; or the foundation of any scholarship may in like manner be vacated.

§ 70. In the selection and transfer of the incumbents of scholarships, other things being equal, preference must always be given to candidates requiring material aid and of decided religious character. Preference.

§ 71. The stipends awarded to the incumbents of Prize Scholarships for undergraduates, may be conferred, at the option of the recipients, either in the form of money or of medals, books or other appropriate tokens of distinguished merit. Stipends of prize scholarships may be in money, or in medals, &c.

§ 72. All the Scholarships that may be founded pursuant to this instrument, shall be numbered; and each shall be distinguished by its appropriate number, and by such additional terms of designation as may be directed by the Trustees of Union College and the Visitors herein appointed. Scholarships to be numbered.

§ 73. The President of Union College, or in case of his death or absence, the Vice President, shall keep a book to receive the subscription of candidates for Auxiliary Scholarships to the pledge hereinafter prescribed. President to keep book for receiving pledge of auxiliary scholars. But no candidate for such Scholarship shall be allowed to subscribe such pledge or to receive any part of the stipend herein provided, until he shall have furnished satisfactory evidence of good moral character, and that he has passed the requisite examination, and that he is fully and thoroughly prepared to enter the class for which he is recommended. Evidence of character to be furnished. Nor may any incumbent of an Auxiliary Scholarship be continued on the foundation to which he has been admitted, any longer than he shall continue to sustain an unblemished moral character and hold an honorable standing in his class, and be punctual in attending Church on the Sabbath, and all the other prescribed College exercises during the week; a report in relation to which particulars must be made to the Visitors by the President or Register, at the time of the examination at the end of each term.

§ 74. The President of Union College shall in like manner receive the pledge hereinafter prescribed, from candidates for Prize Scholarships for undergraduates, who shall have sustained the requisite examination by the committee appointed for that purpose; but no certificate shall be given by such committee except to candidates actually possessing the qualifications hereinbefore prescribed, and of blameless President to receive pledge from candidates for prize scholarships.

Must continue to sustain standing.

moral character; nor can any incumbent of a Prize Scholarship for undergraduates be continued any longer on any foundation to which he has been admitted, than he shall continue to sustain the standing held when admitted, and shall also continue punctually to attend Church on the Sabbath, and all the other prescribed College exercises during the other days of the week, of which report, as aforesaid, shall be made at the close of each term to the Visitors.

Two or more scholarships may be assigned to the same person.

§ 75. Two or more Auxiliary Scholarships or Prize Scholarships for undergraduates, may in the discretion of the President, for special reasons, be assigned to the same incumbent while an undergraduate, or after having been selected a resident graduate.

President may appoint to graduate prize scholarships.

§ 76. The President of Union College, or in case of vacancy in the office of President, the Vice President, may appoint incumbents to the Prize Scholarships, for graduates of Union College, or Fellowships, from among those who were pre-eminent scholars in their respective classes, or young men of eminent attainments (not graduates) who shall sign the pledge required of the Assistant Professors. The incumbents of the graduate Prize Scholarships or Fellows must be unmarried men, reside in College, and besides hearing recitations when required must perform such additional official duties as the President shall prescribe; and an additional compensation may be paid them from the income of the Miscellaneous Fund or any other surplus fund, if the Trustees and Visitors shall so decide; or two or more Scholarships may for special reasons be by them assigned to the same individual.

Must be unmarried men.

Additional compensation may be paid.

§ 77. Candidaties for Auxiliary Scholarships and for Prize Scholarships for undergraduates, can only be admitted to their respective foundations by signing the following Pledge:

Pledge for auxiliary and prize scholarships for undergraduates

§ 78. I, solemnly promise that I will neither use tobacco in any of its forms, nor spirituous liquors, either habitually or occasionally, as a beverage; that I will not join any College Society without the consent and approbation of the President of the College, and that I will punctually attend religious worship on the Sabbath, and the other prescribed exercises of the College on the other days of the week, so long as I shall continue to receive the avails of any Scholarship founded by Eliphalet Nott.

§ 79. And the candidates for Auxiliary Scholarships and Prize Scholarships for undergraduates, who shall have signed the said pledge, shall be admitted to the said Scholarships respectively in the order in which they received their respective certificates from the examiners hereinbefore provided, until the whole number of such Scholarships shall be filled, unless certain candidates in the opinion of the examiners shall have entitled themselves to preference by pre-eminent merit.

Order in which candidates to be admitted.

ARTICLE IX.

IX.

§ 80. Should any differences arise between the Trustees of Union College and the Board of Visitors, in respect to the powers or duties of either, such differences shall be submitted to the Justices of the Supreme Court residing in the district in which Schenectady is situated, whose decision shall be final. And in case of a change in the organization of the Judiciary, then to the Senior Judge of the highest court of law and equity having original jurisdiction in the district in which Schenectady is situated, whose decision shall be final.

Differences how to be settled.

§ 81. As soon as the whole of the trust property shall become productive, and sooner if practicable, the whole number of Auxiliary Scholarships and Prize Scholarships for undergraduates must be filled, if a sufficient number of qualified applicants to fill the same shall offer; and they must continue to be filled so long as this shall continue to be the case. But if at any time there shall not be a sufficient number of qualified applicants to fill such Scholarships, then the stipends of the vacant Scholarships may, in the discretion of the Trustees and Visitors, be applied for the time being to any of the other specified objects in said deed of trust.

Whole number of scholarships to be filled.

§ 82. The continuance of the same paternal government now established in Union College, and the same system of reporting delinquencies by the Professors and other officers, to the President, and of correspondence by him with the parents of delinquents, and of privately dismissing from College, with the least possible injury to the offender, where reformation is hopeless, as is now practised, is earnestly recommended with respect to all the Officers and Pupils in the Institution; and the same is explicitly required with respect to the incumbent of every Professorship, and Assistant Professorship and Scholarship

Paternal government to be continued.

founded by this trust, and it is expressly enjoined on the Visitors to insist thereon.

Execution. § 83. In witness that the foregoing instrument is the voluntary and well-considered act and deed of the said Eliphalet Nott, he has hereunto subscribed his name and affixed his seal, this twenty-eighth day of December, in the year of our Lord one thousand eight hundred and fifty-three.

ELIPH'T. NOTT, [L. S.]

In presence of
L. H. WILLARD.

U. E. Nott's release of rights. § 84. And I, Urania E. Nott, wife of the said Eliphalet Nott, hereby join my husband in the said deed; and in consideration of the uses and purposes for which the said instrument is made, and with the view of aiding and promoting the same; and in further consideration of the sum of One Dollar, to me in hand paid by the Trustees of Union College, in the Town (now city) of Schenectady, in the State of New-York, do hereby grant, convey, release and quit-claim to the said Trustees, all right, interest, estate and claim that I have, or may have, in or to the property, rights and interests described in the foregoing instrument, and therein conveyed to the said College; whether such rights, interest or claim, be for my dower or thirds in the said proproperty, or otherwise.

In witness whereof, I have hereunto set my hand and seal the day and year above written.

URANIA E. NOTT, [L. S.]

In presence of
L. H. WILLARD.

STATE OF NEW-YORK, }
SCHENECTADY COUNTY, } SS.

On this twenty-eighth day of January, A. D., 1854, before me personally appeared Eliphalet Nott and Urania E. his wife, to me known to be the individuals described in, and who executed the foregoing Trust Deed and Schedules attached, and severally acknowledged that they executed the same. And the said Urania E. Nott, on a private examination, separate and apart from her husband, acknowledged that she executed the same freely, and without any fear or compulsion of or from her said husband.

L. H. WILLARD,
Commissioner of Deeds.

www.ingramcontent.com/pod-product-compliance
Lightning Source LLC
LaVergne TN
LVHW011145110826
845150LV00008B/2528
* 9 7 8 1 4 1 8 1 9 2 4 0 2 *